ADVENTURE OUTDOORS

Wild TRAIL

Hiking and Camping

NEIL CHAMPION

W
FRANKLIN WATTS

An Appleseed Editions book

Paperback edition 2014

First published in 2012 by Franklin Watts
338 Euston Road, London NW1 3BH

Franklin Watts Australia
Hachette Children's Books
Level 17/207 Kent St, Sydney, NSW 2000

Created by Appleseed Editions Ltd,
Well House, Friars Hill, Guestling,
East Sussex TN35 4ET

Designed and illustrated by Guy Callaby
Edited by Mary-Jane Wilkins
Photo research by Su Alexander

ISBN 978 14451 3173 3

Dewey Classification: 796.5

All words in **bold** can be found in the Glossary on page 30.

Picture credits
l = left, r = right, c = centre, t = top, b = bottom
Page 1 Thinkstock; 2 Digital Vision/Thinkstock; 4 Polka Dot Images/
Thinkstock; 5t Huansheng Xu/Shutterstock, b BMCL/Shutterstock:
6 & 7t Jupiterimages/Thinkstock , 7b Thinkstock; 8t Stockbyte/Thinkstock,
b Thinkstock; 9t Jupiterimages/Thinkstock, b Wikimedia Commons/Flickr/
Guilhem Vellut; 10t & c Thinkstock, b Jupiterimages/Thinkstock;
11 Shutterstock; 12t Thinkstock, b George Doyle/Thinkstock;
13 Jim Parkin/Shutterstock; 14 Jupiterimages/Thinkstock; 15tl Auremar/
Shutterstock, tr Stockbyte/Thinkstock, b Alexey Stiop/Shutterstock;
16 Igor Plotnikov/Shutterstock; 17 Vitek12/Shutterstock; 20 Hemera
Technologies/Thinkstock; 21 Thinkstock; 22t Thinkstock,
b Thomas Northcut/Thinkstock; 23, 24, 25 & 26 Thinkstock;
27t Ondrej Garaj/Shutterstock, b Nella/Shutterstock; 28 George
Doyle/Thinkstock; 29, 31 & 32t Thinkstock, 32b Creatas/Thinkstock;
Page number image Thinkstock

Front cover: Kapu/Shutterstock

Printed in China

Franklin Watts is a division of
Hachette Children's Books,
an Hachette UK company.
www.hachette.co.uk

Contents

Let's go hiking!

Our planet is a wild place. There are areas to go wild walking and camping everywhere. These are great ways to get close to nature and to get fit. Whether you choose a one-day hike in hills and woods, or a week-long trek carrying your food, tent and sleeping gear, there's a world of adventure waiting for you.

Amazing FACTS

A British long-distance walker once walked all the way from the southernmost tip of South America to the most northerly point in Alaska. His name was George Meegan and he covered a staggering 30,608 km. His journey took 2,425 days – that's just over six and a half years – starting in 1977 and finishing in 1983!

Carrying all they need for a camping expedition, these hikers have the freedom of the hills before them.

TRUE Survivors

Every year people run into trouble in remote places. Some are prepared, but others are thrown unexpectedly into danger. This happened to Ricky Megee in April 2006 in a remote part of the Australian outback. His car broke down on the border of Northern Territory and Western Australia. Ricky managed to survive for 71 days on a diet of leeches, frogs, lizards and grasshoppers before he stumbled out of the bush and was rescued. He said: "I ate the leeches raw... the only thing I really... had to cook was the frogs. I slipped them on to a bit of wire and stuck the wire on top of my [shelter], let the sun dry them out a fair bit until they were a bit crispy and then just ate them." He was lucky that it was the rainy season so he had enough water. He lost more than half his body weight during his ordeal. Mark Clifford, who found him, reported that he was a walking skeleton.

Taking up the challenge

Before you start, you need to learn the skills which will allow you to stay safe, such as finding the way, getting fit for the hike, first aid, how to choose a campsite and how to read the weather.

Getting started

There are walking and hiking clubs all round the world, so there should be one near you. A school outdoor pursuits club is the ideal place to learn about hiking. Make sure you learn from older and more experienced people, starting with local walks and building up to more adventurous expeditions.

Studying a map and looking at where you will be hiking are important preparation.

Learning to hike

You might think that walking skills are automatic, but it's a good idea to learn to walk efficiently on all sorts of terrain – steep hills, boulders, slopes covered in scree (loose stones) or rough woodland tracks. Every time you stumble, you waste energy correcting your balance. Efficient walking takes time and effort, but can be learned close to home, in a park, along a river bank or even on the street. Wear the boots or trainers you plan to use on longer hikes to get used to them and break them in.

Here are some top tips.

- Land on your heel and roll forward on to your toes.

- Don't take big strides, just the length that feels natural and comfortable.

- Stand up straight, but not rigidly.

- Swing your arms forward and back for momentum.

- Use your back leg for power rather than the leading leg.

- When walking up a steep hill don't get out of breath – you need to be able to talk and walk at the same time.

A mountain rescue team helps an injured hill walker.

Amazing FACTS

Humans walk more efficiently than any other mammal. We use the whole of each foot, landing on the heel and moving forward to spring off the toes in a naturally stable movement. This is because humans have a large heel compared with animals, as well as a big toe next to our other toes to help us balance.

Mountain rescue services

Every year thousands of walkers get into trouble round the world. In the area of Snowdonia in Wales, an average of 150 people are injured, and about ten people are killed, every year. Mountain rescue services were set up to help people in difficulty. Today, helicopters, teams of experienced rescuers and even highly trained dogs, all stand ready to leap into action and help prevent tragedy.

Hiking kit

You need the right kit for active walking: lightweight and cool in hot climates, or warm when it's cold. Don't forget your hands, feet and head. You lose a lot of heat from your head, so wear a hat to stay warm.

side pockets give fast access

A well packed rucksack.

The layering system
Wear lots of thin layers, rather than one or two thick ones. This tried and trusted method keeps you comfortable in all types of weather.

Base layer
Wear clothes made of cotton or artificial fibres in warm weather and wool or artificial fibres in the cold (including underwear, socks, long johns, T-shirts and shirts).

Mid layer
This is a layer to put on when the temperature drops (eg a sweatshirt, fleece or jumper).

Shell clothing
This outer layer protects you from wind, rain and snow. Modern fabrics keep rain out, but allow sweat to pass through so you stay dry underneath.

Hiking in cold or snowy weather may mean wearing all your layers of clothing.

Footwear

You need boots which give you ankle support for high mountain treks and long distance hikes. Boots also last longer than lighter footwear. Trainers are great for low to mid-level walks as they are lighter.

TRUE Survivors

Nanga Parbat

Heinrich Harrer (1912-2006) was an Austrian mountaineer and sportsman. In 1939 he was in British India to climb one of the world's highest mountains, Nanga Parbat, when the Second World War began, and he was taken prisoner by the British. In April 1944, after several attempts, he escaped and began an epic walk through the Himalayas to Tibet.

It took Heinrich two years to reach Lhasa, the capital, crossing high passes such as the Tsang Chok-La (5,896m) and enduring snowstorms and sub-zero temperatures. He had only the clothes in which he escaped, and by the time he arrived in Lhasa he was in rags. He wrote a book about his adventures, called *Seven Years in Tibet*, which was made into a film starring Brad Pitt in 1997.

Camping kit

If you go camping with a car, you can take a large tent and lots of gear, but if you are backpacking, you need less weight: a small tent, cooking stove and few clothes.

Choosing a tent

The lighter a tent is, the more expensive it will be. A good backpacking tent for one or two people should weigh two kilos or less. If you camp at a low level in summer, any shape will do, but camping high in the mountains you might encounter storms, so you need a stable tent in a **geodesic** shape.

A geodesic tent (top) is more stable than a traditional ridge tent (above).

Amazing FACTS

Some modern tents can withstand winds of up to 160 km/h. Their geodesic design makes them very stable.

What sort of cooker?

You can take just a steel and a flint, or matches to make a fire, but make sure that you will be able to find kindling and wood for fuel. Some national parks and campsites don't allow wood fires as they use up natural resources and can spread. You can take a burner that runs on gas, meths or petrol.

Camp cooking in the snow.

Kit list

- Rucksack (60-85 litres)
- Tent
- Sleeping mat
- Sleeping bag and liner
- Cooker, fuel and matches
- Shell clothing
- Spare socks and underwear
- Warm clothing (+ hat and gloves)
- Food
- Water bottle
- First aid kit
- Emergency whistle

TRUE Survivors

One night in the winter of 1986, some mountain leader students were sleeping in **snow holes** high in the Cairngorm Mountains in Scotland, with three mountaineers from the National Outdoor Centre. None of them knew that one of the most violent storms to hit these mountains was about to kick off. Radio contact with base in the morning told them to expect strong winds of 160 km/h, which would make walking and navigating difficult. But as the day went on, the winds strengthened, until by early afternoon there were gusts of over 350 km/h. The climbers were blown off their feet and sent 20 metres across the snowy plateau. They could hardly breathe as the wind was so powerful. They became split up, but, amazingly, all the students managed to crawl off the mountain and down into the valley to reach help.

Thinking about safety

Safety is key when planning a hike. Does everyone have the right kit and know how to use it? Do you have enough food and water, an emergency kit and a plan if you have to cut the trip short?

Planning ahead

You need to know what to do if things go wrong. A plan of action saves time and helps prevent panic. Go on a basic first aid course and make sure you leave a route card with someone responsible. Then if you are late returning to base, a rescue team will know where to find you. A **route card** also helps you think about the possible hazards in the area you are going to (a river, cliffs, marshy ground or dense forest).

Hikers should know how to deal with minor injuries such as a cut knee.

Filling in a route card helps you focus on the planned hike. It is also part of your safety planning.

Route Plan

- To be completed in accordance with Policy, Organisation and Rules.
- Take a copy with you and leave a copy with a responsible local person – cancel on return.

Date: 20/11/12 DAY....... OF...... OR ONE DAY Maps Used: OS Landranger 160 (1:50,000)

Magnetic Variation: 2°

Objective *Summit of Pen y Fan*

Place or Grid Reference	Magnetic Bearing	Distance (km)	Height Gained (m)	Description of Route	Est. Time for Leg	Total Time
START *Car Park* 025 249				*Steep up hill*	20 mins	20 mins
TO *Path junction*	168°	500m	110m	*Pass crags on left*	21 mins	41 mins
TO *Stream junction*	208°	700m	70m	*Down to col then up*	20 mins	61 mins
TO *Crest of ridge*	216°	600m	80m	*Follow ridge to top*	63 mins	124 mins
TO *Summit of PyF* 012 216	200°	2000m	230m			
TO						
TO						
TO						
TO						
TO						
TOTALS						

Add 10 minutes per hour for safety

START TIME

FINISH TI...
REACH CAMP...

Escape Routes

(1) From ....

Return by ascent route

(2) From ....

(3) From ....

WEATHER FORECAST

WIND:
Speed/force *16 kph, gusts up to 33 kph*
Direction *south-westerly* becoming *56 kph, gusts up to 80 kph* at .... metres

TEMPERATURE
Sea level .... *14* .... °C becoming .... at .... metres
Cloud base *650* .... metres .... *7* .... °C at *700* metres

OUTLOOK: *An improving picture as the day progresses, with temperatures rising by a degree or two by mid afternoon. The day will remain dry, though visibility will be poor in the cloud.*

EQUIPMENT IN PARTY

THIS LIST I... ...ED TO BE A COMPLETE ONE OF ALL THE EQUIPMENT (BOTH PERSONAL AND ...BUT MORE TO GIVE OTHERS AN INDICATION OF HOW THE PARTY IS EQUIPPED SH... CARRIED BY EACH MEMBER O... ...E AN EMERGENCY. ITEMS MARKED * SHOULD BE THE EQUIPMENT WILL BE DEPENDE... ...UR OBJECTIVE AND THE DURATION OF THE JOURNEY).

Insert numbers if appropriate:
.... Maps (minimum of 2)
.... Compasses (minimum of 2)
.... *Waterproofs
.... *Spare Clothing
.... *Whistle
.... *Food/Drink (for journey)
.... First Aid Kit
.... Watch
.... Emergency Rations
.... Survival Bag(s) or Tent
.... *Ice Axe /...

EMERGENCIES

Note:

These notes are for those in the local area who have been handed a copy of this Route Plan. If the party fails to return by the agreed time please contact those listed below.

1 Home Contact
Name *Bryn Hammond*
Address *26 Cambria Road*
Talgarth, Brecon, Powys
Telephone *01874 721467*

2 Home Contact
Name *Jake Turnbull*
Add ....

DID YOU KNOW?

Six top reasons that people get into trouble and need to be rescued.

- Not knowing how to navigate and getting lost.

- Not taking a map and compass.

- Not having the right clothing (waterproofs or warm gear).

- Not knowing when to turn back.

- Trying a hike that is too hard.

- Injuries: mostly knee or ankle injuries from stumbling on a trail.

A search and rescue team on duty in the Rocky Mountains.

TRUE
Survivors

In November 2009, two young men set off for a day's hunting in the mountains of the west coast of the USA. They knew the area and took emergency gear: mobile phones, a GPS, matches and lighters, but no sleeping gear. High up they came across unexpected deep snow, but carried on regardless. Soon they were suffering from hypothermia They were lucky to stumble across some dead trees, which they set alight to keep warm overnight.

The following morning they were rescued because their parents had alerted the authorities.

How could the two men have planned better? They could have taken better emergency equipment: bivy bags, sleeping bags and extra food. They could have taken better clothing. One was wearing cotton jeans, which gave no warmth, but soaked up water and sweat, making him colder. They could have turned back when they hit deep snow, instead of battling on to the hunting ground.

Learning to navigate

Navigation is the most important skill a hiker needs to learn. This includes knowing how to use a compass and read a map, and also being able to study the landscape and choose a good route across it.

Using a map

Maps represent what you see on the ground, scaled down to a smaller size. They use symbols to represent buildings, forests, cliffs, and so on.

The top of a map always points to **grid north**, but navigators use three norths: **magnetic**, **true** and grid.

Contour lines on a hiking map represent 10m, 15m or 20m in vertical distance (height).

Grid squares on a map are usually one kilometre square.

The most useful **map scales** for walking are 1:25,000 and 1:50,000.

To orientate your map, you can line up features on the map with the features you see around you, or use your compass. Place the compass on the map and line up the north-south arrow with the north-south grid lines on the map.

Amazing FACTS

Orienteering is a sport that combines running with navigation. Competitors find their way around a course using a map and compass to reach control points. One type, called Rogaining, involves running and navigating for up to 24 hours non-stop over difficult wild terrain.

Knowing your compass

A compass has a magnetic arrow, the red end of which always points to magnetic north. There is also an arrow showing the direction to travel in, grid lines and a ruler on the base plate. You need to learn how to use these different parts of the compass to orientate your map and take a **bearing**.

TRUE Survivors

In 1971, 17-year-old Juliane Köpcke was on a flight to Peru. The plane was struck by lightning and exploded, killing everyone on board except Juliane, who fell to earth still strapped in her seat. She found herself in dense rainforest, but kept her head and remembered some advice from her father – find a stream and follow it downstream to find human **habitation**. She waded downstream for nine days, eventually finding a canoe and shelter where she was discovered and rescued. During her journey she had plenty to drink but very little to eat. Her rescuers took her on a seven-hour canoe ride to the nearest timber mill, from which she was airlifted to hospital to recover from her ordeal.

More about navigation

Experienced navigators have plenty of strategies to help them when a trip doesn't go according to plan. Here are some of them.

Handrails and how to use them

A handrail is a long, continuous feature marked on a map and easy to find on the ground. Examples include fences, streams and rivers, roads and well-used footpaths. You can follow them easily and mark your progress on the map. Imagine your tent is in a patch of wild ground. Close by is a river – say 50 metres away – where a fence meets the river bank. You come back after dark because your hike that day took longer than planned. Instead of trying to navigate across open country in the dark hoping to find your tent, you navigate to the river. You then use the river as a handrail to find the fence. From there you can take a bearing and walk the 50m to your tent. Where the fence meets the river is your attack point.

Left The river would provide a useful handrail to help find this tent in darkness.

Top tips for when you're lost

1 Don't panic.

2 Take time to think; don't rush decisions.

3 Recall the landscape you have just walked over. Did you cross a river, climb steeply, or did you walk through woodland? Try to find features you remember on your map. You might be able to **relocate** yourself.

4 Can you see any big features around you? Try to find them on the map.

5 Think back to the point where you last knew your position. Try to work out how you can get back to that point.

Navigation off the summit of a mountain should not be a problem in clear weather. It is much more difficult in the dark or in low cloud.

Amazing FACTS

The top of Ben Nevis (1,344m) is the highest point in Britain. The average annual rainfall is more than four metres, with only one clear day in every ten, and an average annual temperature of -1°Celsius. Gales scream across the summit for 260 days a year. Navigating off the top in poor visibility is one of the hardest tests in mountain climbing and the notorious Five Finger Gully claims those who get it wrong. Several people die there every year, including university lecturer George Gibson, who fell into it in February 1994.

Getting fit

Hiking helps to make you fit and the more you do, the fitter you become. You can prepare yourself for long hikes by doing some simple training and you also need know how to warm up and warm down.

Warming up

Anyone taking part in a sport will benefit from warming up beforehand. A warm up raises your heart rate and warms your muscles and tendons ready for exercise. Start with simple jogging or skipping; you can go for a run or gently jog on the spot for ten minutes. This gets your heart and lungs pumping blood and oxygen around your body. Follow with some simple **dynamic stretches**, such as a shoulder and arm stretch, hip stretch, pelvis rotation and upper back rotation.

1. Shoulder and arm stretch Bring one arm across your chest and hold it there with your other arm.

2. Hip stretch Stand with your feet slightly apart, with your hands on your hips. Swing your hips round four times clockwise, then four times anticlockwise.

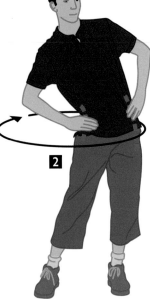

3 Hip and thigh stretch Take a large step forward and hold it for three seconds, then step and hold with the other leg. Make four big strides, two with each leg.

TRUE Survivors

Slawomir Rawicz (1915-2004) was in the Polish army when he was captured by the Russians and imprisoned in Siberia. He escaped in 1941 and walked 6,500 km through some of the most hostile terrain in the world – including the Gobi Desert, across Tibet and over the Himalayas. He arrived in British India in 1942. He had survived extreme cold, hunger and danger from bandits to claim his freedom and a place in the record books for one of the longest and toughest walks ever.

Warming down

Always warm down after exercise. This means doing some **static stretches** and holding each stretch for at least 20 seconds. A warm down helps muscles repair themselves after exercise. Useful stretches include: shoulder stretch, hamstring stretch, thigh stretch, hip stretch and calf stretch.

1

Amazing FACTS

Our bodies adapt to the demands we make on them. As you hike and train, your heart and lungs gradually grow bigger and stronger. This means that oxygen travels more efficiently around your body. You can even grow more **capillaries**. These tiny blood vessels help to cool you down when you exercise hard. Your body will grow muscle to give you more strength and your **metabolism** changes to sustain you through a long day of walking.

*1. **Thigh stretch** Stand on one foot, holding on to something for balance if you need to. Pull your other foot up behind you and hold it there for 20 seconds. Do this three times with each foot.*

2

*2. **Hamstring stretch** Bend forward at the waist. Put your right foot out in front of you with your toes raised. Bend your left knee slightly. Hold this for 20 seconds then swap legs. Do two stretches for each leg.*

3

*3. **Calf stretch** Put your right leg in front of you and press your hands against something solid, such as a wall or tree. Keep both feet flat on the ground as you lean forward. Hold for 20 seconds then swap legs.*

Planning an expedition

Walking and camping in the wild tests your **self-reliance** and skills. Start planning by researching the area, then work out how long to go for, where to find water and what you will eat.

Amazing FACTS

The human body is mostly water, which makes up more than 60 per cent of our weight. Water keeps our bodies working – digesting food, providing energy, helping the brain function. You can survive without food for a couple of weeks, but without water for only two or three days in hot weather. The harder you work, the more water you need, because you lose water when you sweat. When hiking you might need two or three litres before reaching camp.

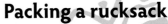

Make sure you have a water purification system in areas where water may carry bugs.

Packing a rucksack

Make sure your rucksack fits you well and can hold all you need. This is likely to be a tent, sleeping bag, mat, cooker and fuel, food, cutlery and bowl, matches or lighter, hat and gloves, waterproofs, spare clothes, first aid kit, toiletries, torch, map and compass, and maybe a mobile phone and **GPS**. You can share some equipment. Don't carry more than a quarter of your own weight – 12-18 kg. Put items you will need while walking in the outer pockets. Pack fuel away from food and distribute the weight evenly.

The route

Make sure you can find running water for washing, drinking and cooking. Find out how pure it is and take purification tablets if necessary. Two nights away might be enough for a first trip. Remember, you won't be able to walk so far with a heavy rucksack, so make sure you are realistic when planning where to stop for the night.

The northern Sahara Desert in Morocco is one of the most hostile places on Earth. Hikers need special training to cope with desert expeditions.

TRUE Survivors

One of the toughest foot races in the world is the Marathon des Sables. It takes place in the desert in Morocco, North Africa, and competitors cover 233 km over six days. In 1994, Italian Mauro Prosperi became lost in a sandstorm a few days after the race began. Within 36 hours he had run out of food and water. During the day, the temperature rose to almost 50°C. Mauro managed to survive for nine days by drinking the blood of the bats and snakes that live in the desert, and was eventually found by local nomads. He was nearly 300 km off course.

Where to go

There are many exciting places to go hiking, including forests, hills and mountains, deserts and coasts. All these places can be hazardous in different ways.

Hills and mountains

Steep climbs are tough going so you need to be fit before you start. There is often cloud, rain or snow over high ground, so you will need the right clothes. Temperatures drop between one and two degrees Celsius for every 100 metres you climb and winds can be two or three times stronger on summits than in valleys.

Above *A peaceful walk along a beautiful coastline.* **Below** *Morning mist over still waters and woods.*

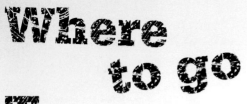

Rivers and marshes

Wet regions are full of wildlife and bogs can be a major hazard. They can be dangerous to cross, so you may need to make a long detour around them. Rivers can rise quickly, especially if they are in or near mountains. Heavy rain high up, many kilometres from where you are, can make streams swollen and impassable. Make sure you know where the bridges are and that you get a weather forecast.

Desert hikes

Deserts are demanding landscapes to walk through. Always carry plenty of water and know where the next clean water source is. Get up early to walk in the cool morning and rest in the shade during the hottest part of the day. Cover up with light, loose clothing but take warm clothes for the nights, which can be cold.

TRUE Survivors

In June 1996, five scouts and three leaders set off into the Grand Canyon, USA. They were going into remote, waterless terrain where temperatures reach over 38°C at midday. They had prepared well, but only three days into their trip, they ran out of water far from any source. Their situation quickly became desperate and one of the scouts died of **heat exhaustion** and **dehydration**. The others were eventually rescued, having reached the river at the bottom of the canyon when a group of paddlers came by. Once alerted, rescue services sent helicopters to fly them to safety.

Amazing FACTS

There are deserts on every continent and they cover about a quarter of the Earth's surface. The Sahara and Gobi are hot deserts and Antarctica is a cold one. The highest temperature ever recorded was 58°C in Libya, North Africa, in September 1922. Temperatures can drop 50°C between day and night.

Watch the weather

You need to know the weather forecast for the area you plan to hike in. There is accurate information on the internet, as well as on television, radio and in newspapers. You should also be able to read the weather by looking at clouds and working out wind direction.

TRUE Survivors

In the summer of 2004, four mountaineers were trapped in their tents on the highest mountain in Western Europe – Mount Blanc. On the third day, they heard screams outside. 'I opened the zip of the tent to find a man babbling hysterically. We dragged him inside, wrapped him in foil blankets and gave him water. As he recovered, he told us his story. His climbing companion had died in the storm and he had staggered around for 12 hours before finding our footprints in yesterday's snow leading him to our tent.' When the storm died down, the team alerted the emergency services who sent a helicopter for the injured man. The four mountaineers then walked down to the valley in fine weather. Would knowing that the storm was forecast have allowed them to avoid three frightening days trapped in their tents and saved the life of another climber?

Reading clouds

Clouds are one of the best indicators of the weather that is coming your way. High cirrus clouds may mean that a **cold front** will arrive in six to eighteen hours, depending on the wind speed. This will bring rain and maybe poor visibility and strong winds. There are many types of cloud, with names such as altocumulus, nimbostratus and cumulonimbus. They can all give you clues about the weather, so learn some of the common types that occur in your area.

A raging river in full flood is a frightening and very dangerous hazard in the wild.

Floods, storms and heat waves

Knowing in advance that bad weather is on the way can make a difference to planning. If it rains heavily stay away from rivers and flood plains. When thunder and lightning are about keep away from summits, ridges and wide open ground. If the forecast is for a heat wave, make sure you plan a hike where there is shade (in a forest, for example) and take plenty of water.

Stratus

Cirrus

Altocumulus

Cumulus

Long distance trails

All around the world there are fantastic long distance trails to walk. Some take weeks to complete, but you don't need to cover the whole trail. You can choose to walk for a day, a weekend, or maybe a week.

Apollo Bay, south west of Melbourne, where the Great Ocean Walk begins.

North America

The Appalachian Trail This famous trek goes down the east coast of America, from Maine to Georgia. It is just over 3,500 km long, and would take around 175 days to cover.

The Colorado Trail This goes from Waterton Canyon near Denver to Durango. It is 777 km long and rarely goes below 3000m, reaching a high point of just over 4,000m, so is only for experienced hikers.

The Rideau Trail This trail runs from Cataraqui Bay in Kingston, Ontario, in Canada, 387 km to the Ottawa River, Ontario.

Durango in Mesa Verde National Park, at the end of the dramatic Colorado Trail.

104 KM

Australia and New Zealand

Abel Tasman Coast Track This hike in New Zealand goes from Marahau to Wainui on South Island. It is 51 km long and takes three to five days. About 200,000 people a year walk this trail, and it's suitable for beginners.

Great Ocean Walk This trail is in the state of Victoria. It starts at Apollo Bay about 200 km south west of Melbourne. It is 104 km long, finishing at Glenample Homestead, and takes about a week to walk.

Europe

The West Highland Way This 154 km trail starts just north of Glasgow, at Milngavie and ends about eight days later at Fort William. About 85,000 hikers a year pass over remote Rannoch Moor and drop down into Glen Coe. The last stage passes the foot of Ben Nevis, the highest mountain in Britain.

E4 European Long-Distance Path This monster trek is more than 10,000 km long and runs from Spain in the west to Bulgaria and Greece in the east. On the island of Crete, the E4 takes in the high mountains of Lefki Ori and the highest point of Mount Psiloritis.

The West Highland Way passes close to Glen Coe, one of the finest mountain areas in Scotland.

154 KM

What do you know about hiking?

Do you think you're ready to take on the challenge of following the trail into the wilderness? Could you find your way across unknown country using a map and compass? Could you pack all the right things for a weekend camping trip away from all the home comforts? Try this quiz to find out just how much you know about the great outdoors. The answers are on page 31.

1 Which is correct?
Efficient walking means:
a Taking big strides
b Walking toe first, then heel
c Using your back leg to get power moving forward, rather than your front leg
d Swinging your arms to help move forward
e Stooping

3 Cirrus clouds high in the sky mean that there is a cold front approaching.
True or false?

2 The layering system is:
a A way of packing your rucksack so that everything inside is neat and tidy
b Wearing several thin layers of clothing rather than one or two thick ones
c A way of making a cake when camping
d A cloud formation

4 Which items would you not take on a weekend wild camping expedition?
a Tent
b Sleeping bag
c Slippers
d Spare cutlery
e Playstation portable
f Cooker

5 A route card is:

a A special playing card used by hikers for entertainment when camping

b A form you fill in giving details of your group, where you are going to hike and camp, and when you will return

c A type of map that shows you where to walk

d A type of credit card

▼ **6** Name these stretches.

1
2
3
4
5
6

7 How many different types of north are mentioned in this book?

a 3
b 7
c 10
d 18
e none

8 When hiking in a hot desert, you should wear tight-fitting clothing.

9 On average, as you walk higher up a mountain, the temperature will go down by:

a 10-15°C every 100m higher you go
b 10-15°C every 150m higher you go
c 1-2°C every 100m higher you go
d It stays the same whatever your height

10 If you get lost, what should you do?

a Panic
b Take time and don't rush into a decision
c Try to remember where you last knew your position on the map
d Run in a circle to find where you are
e Put your map away, as it didn't prevent you getting lost in the first place

Glossary

bearing Finding the direction you want to go in using your compass is called taking a bearing.

capillaries Very small blood vessels that form a network through the body.

cold front The front edge of a colder mass of air moving in to replace warmer air. Where the cold and warm air meet, clouds form and rain falls.

dehydration Losing liquid from the body, for example when you sweat, but don't drink anything. It is a very serious condition and can kill.

dynamic stretches Moving the arms, legs, head and back to warm up the joints.

geodesic A geodesic tent has a dome shape that is very stable. Poles cross over each other to allow the tent to withstand very high winds and shed snow.

GPS A Global Positioning System is a hand-held device that you use to find out where you are and to navigate. It fixes on three or more satellites as they orbit the Earth.

grid north The north that maps point to. It varies from magnetic north in the UK by about two degrees.

grid square Hiking maps are criss-crossed by grid lines that run north-south and east-west. They form squares that are one km square in the UK and Europe.

habitation A term for places where humans live – villages, towns or cities.

heat exhaustion A very serious condition in which someone loses too much water and salt from the body. This is usually a result of exercising hard in very hot conditions.

magnetic north The north to which all magnetized things point, including the needle in a compass.

metabolism All the chemical and physical processes that allow our bodies to function properly – to give us energy, repair our cells, grow and remove waste.

navigation The skill of being able to find your way around using a map and compass, a GPS and natural signs such as the position of the sun and moon, and vegetation.

relocate The skill of finding where you are again once you have been lost.

scale The scale of a map is the relationship between the size of something on a map and its size in the real world. At a scale of 1:25,000, 4 cm on a map represents 1 km on the ground.

self-reliance Being able to look after yourself, especially in stressful or tricky situations.

snow hole A shelter dug into a bank of snow big enough to sleep in.

static stretches Stretches held for 20-30 seconds which you do after exercise.

tendon A strong band of tissue that connects muscles to bones.

true north The point on the globe where scientifically worked out north lies (as opposed to magnetic north or grid north).

Websites

www.thebmc.co.uk The British Mountaineering Council

www.ramblers.org.uk The Ramblers Association

www.americanhiking.org The American Hiking Society

www.hikingandbackpacking.com The American and Canadian backpacking association

www.backcountrynz.com The New Zealand hiking website

www.aussiehiking.com The Australian website for hikers

Books

Hiking Jacques Marais, New Holland Publishers, 2002
Essential Tips: Hiking Hugh McManners, Dorling Kindersley, 2000
Orienteering Neil Champion, Wayland Publishers, 2008
Finding Your Way Neil Champion, Franklin Watts, 2010

Quiz answers

1 *c and d*
2 *b*
3 *True*
4 *c, d and e*
5 *b*

6 *1 Thigh stretch*
2 Hamstring stretch
3 Shoulder stretch
4 Calf stretch
5 Hip stretch
6 Hip and thigh stretch

7 *a*
8 *False*
9 *c*
10 *b and c*

Index